# ENFP PERSONALITY - DISCOVER YOUR STRENGTHS AND THRIVE AS A CHAMPION

*THE ULTIMATE GUIDE TO THE ENFP PERSONALITY TYPE INCLUDING: ENFP CAREERS, ENFP PERSONALITY TRAITS, ENFP RELATIONSHIPS, AND FAMOUS ENFPS*

*FIND HEALTH, WEALTH, AND HAPPINESS AS AN ENFP*

DAN JOHNSTON

Copyright © 2013, by Dan Johnston. All Rights Reserved.

No part of this publication may be reproduced, distributed, or transmitted in any form or by any means, including photocopying, recording, or other electronic or mechanical methods, or by any information storage and retrieval system without the prior written permission of the publisher, except in the case of very brief quotations embodied in critical reviews and certain other non-commercial uses permitted by copyright law.

Myers-Briggs Type Indicator, Myers-Briggs, and MBTI are trademarks or registered trademarks of the MBTI® Trust, Inc., in the United States and other countries.

Published by Dan Johnston

www.DreamsAroundTheWorld.com

# CONTENTS

Why You Should Read This Book ........................................ 5

Free Reader-Only Exclusives: Workbook and Bonuses ....... 9

Disclaimer .............................................................................. 10

Introduction To This series ................................................... 11

Advice From ENFPs for ENFPs............................................ 13

Introduction To Myers-Briggs® ............................................. 17

The 16 types and 4 Groups................................................... 19

    What The Four Letters Mean........................................... 19

    The Four Groups ............................................................. 23

ENFP's Four Functions ......................................................... 25

    How We Use Our Functions............................................ 27

    Connecting With The Past ............................................... 28

Discovering The Champion: Who Is An ENFP?................... 31

In Good Company: Famous ENFPS ..................................... 33

    Famous ENFPs................................................................ 33

    Going Deeper Exercise................................................... 36

Your Secret Weapons ........................................................... 37

    An ENFP's Secret Weapons............................................ 38

    Keys To Using Your Strengths As An ENFP:................... 40

    Going Deeper Exercise................................................... 41

Your Kryptonite ...................................................................... 43

    Shiny Object Syndrome .................................................. 45

Overcoming Your Weaknesses ......................................... 46

Going Deeper Exercise ................................................... 48

**Ideal Career Options For An ENFP** ................................. 49

Popular Professions For ENFPs ...................................... 51

Going Deeper Exercise ................................................... 54

**Thriving At Work** ............................................................. 55

Three Foundations For Thriving At Work ....................... 55

Going Deeper Exercise ................................................... 58

**Rich and Happy Relationships** ..................................... 59

ENFPs In Relationships ................................................... 59

ENFPs' Ideal Matches ...................................................... 60

Tips For Dating As An ENFP ............................................ 61

Tips For Dating An ENFP ................................................. 62

**Keys To Wealth, Health, Happiness, and Success** ............. 65

Practical Solutions To Common Challenges .................. 69

**Next Steps** ...................................................................... 71

**Suggestions and Feedback** .............................................. 72

**A Small Favor** .................................................................. 73

**Other Books on ENFPs' and ENFPs' Best Matches: INTJs and INFJs** ........................................................................ 75

**Books In The Thrive Personality Type Series** .................. 77

**About The Author** ........................................................... 81

**Never Settle – A Short Story** .......................................... 83

iv

# WHY YOU SHOULD READ THIS BOOK

You know those people for whom everything just seems so easy?

Their career or business is always getting better. Their relationships appear happy and fulfilling. They have a satisfying home life, work life, and, by damn, never seem to have a complaint in the world. **Let's call these people the "Thrivers."**

Then there are those for whom life feels like a constant upward swim. At work, they feel like they don't belong. Their relationships are either problematic or unsatisfying. To them, life has always been a struggle. Let's call them the Strugglers.

What's going on here? Are some of us just blessed with good fortune? Is everyone else just cursed with constant struggle?

Don't worry, there are no magical forces at work - just some psychology. It has been my experience that there is only one difference between the Strugglers and the Thrivers.

The Thrivers, by reflection, study, or just dumb luck, have built their lives around their natural personalities. Their work utilizes their strengths while their relationships complement their weaknesses.

A small percentage of the Thrivers came into their lives "naturally." The careers their parents or teachers recommended were the perfect fit for them, or they had a gut feeling that turned out to be right. They met their ideal partner who complemented them perfectly. I believe, however, that this group is the minority.

Most Thrivers have spent years "watching" themselves and reflecting about who they really are. For some, this is a natural process. For others, myself included, it is more of a deliberate process. We read, studied, questioned, and took every test we could find, all in the name of self-awareness. We've made it a priority to know and understand ourselves.

Whatever a Thriver learns about themselves, they use to make significant changes in their lives. They change careers, end relationships, and start new hobbies. They do all this so that one day their lives will be fulfilled and will have a natural flow to it. They do it all to create the life where they will thrive.

This book is for Thrivers: past, present, and future.

If you once had your flow but can't seem to find it again, read on.

If you're in your flow and want to keep and improve it, read on.

And, if you're one of the beautiful souls struggling but committed to finding your flow and to thrive, you're in the right place. Read on.

Today you may feel like a salmon swimming upstream, but this is a temporary state. One day soon, you will find yourself evolving. Perhaps into a dolphin, swimming among those with whom you belong, free to be yourself, to play and to enjoy life. Maybe you'd rather find your place as a whale - wise and powerful, roaming the oceans and setting your own path, respected and admired by all.

## Knowledge Brings Awareness and Awareness Brings Success

I'm an entrepreneur as well as a writer. As an entrepreneur, negotiation plays a big part in any success I might have. One of the secrets to being a good negotiator is always to be the one in the room with the most information.

The same holds true for decision making in our personal lives. When it comes to the big things in life, we can't make a good decision if we don't have all the relevant information.

## WHY YOU SHOULD READ THIS BOOK

I think most of us understand this on an external level. When we're shopping for a new car, we research our options. The prices, the engines, and the warranties. We find out as much as we can to help make our decision.

Unfortunately, we often forget the most important factor in our decisions: Us.

A Ford Focus is a better economic decision and a more enjoyable drive than an SUV...but that doesn't matter if you're 7 feet tall or have 5 kids who need to be driven to hockey in the snow.

When it comes to life decisions, such as our work or relationships, who we are is the most important decision factor.

It doesn't matter if all your friends say he is the perfect guy; it only matters if he's perfect for you. It doesn't matter if your family wants you to be a lawyer, a doctor, or an accountant.... What do you want to do?

IF YOU MAKE YOUR DECISION BASED ON WHAT THE OUTSIDE WORLD SAYS, YOU WON'T FIND THE LEVELS OF HAPPINESS OR FULFILLMENT YOU DESIRE.

In order to make the best decisions, you must first know yourself. That is the purpose of this book: to provide the most in-depth, most relevant information on the ENFP personality type available anywhere.

**By reading this book you will:**

- Improve self-awareness.
- Uncover your natural strengths.
- Understand your weaknesses.
- Discover new career opportunities.
- Learn how to have better relationships.
- Develop a greater understanding of your family, partner, and friends.
- Have the knowledge to build your ideal life around your natural personality.
- Have more happiness, health, love, money, and all around life success while feeling more focused and fulfilled.

# FREE READER-ONLY EXCLUSIVES: WORKBOOK AND BONUSES

When I wrote this book, I set out to create the most *useful* guide available. I know there will always be bigger or more detailed textbooks out there, but how many of them are actually helpful?

To help you get the most from this book, I have created a collection of free extras to support you along the way. To download these, simply visit the special section of my website: www.PersonalityTypesTraining.com/thrive

You will be asked to enter your email address so I can send you the "Thriving Bonus Pack." You'll receive:

1. A 5-part mini-course (delivered via email) with tips on how to optimize your life so you can maximize your strengths and thrive.
2. A compatibility chart showing how you are most likely to relate to the other 15 personality types. You'll discover which people are likely to become good friends (or better) and whom you should avoid at all cost.
3. A PDF workbook to ramp up the results you'll get from this book. It's formatted to be printed, so you can fill in your answers to the exercises in each chapter as you go.

To download the Thriving Bonus Pack, visit:

www.PersonalityTypesTraining.com/thrive

# DISCLAIMER

I know this book will serve you well in discovering your strengths and building your self-awareness. I have researched and written this book based on years of practical experience including running multiple businesses, talking to dozens of people about their strengths and weaknesses, and applying this knowledge to my own life to discover my strengths and build a business around what I do best. With that said, I must emphasize that I am not a psychologist, psychiatrist, or counselor, or in any way qualified to offer medical advice. The information in this book is intended to improve your life but it does not replace professional advice in any way, nor is it legal, medical, or psychiatric advice. So, if you're in a bad place or may be suffering from a mental illness, please seek professional help!

# INTRODUCTION TO THIS SERIES

The goal is this series is to provide a clear window into the strengths, weaknesses, opportunities, and challenges of each type.

You'll discover new things about yourself and find new ways to tap into your strengths and create a life where you thrive. I want you to have every advantage possible in the areas of work, play, relationships, health and finance.

This book is part of a series; each one focuses on one "type." You will find that I write directly to you, although I do not make an assumption as to your personality type or your traits. I will generally refer to the type, aka ENFP, instead of saying "you." Not every trait of a specific type applies to everyone of that type, and we never want to make any assumptions about who you are or about your limitations.

I would recommend beginning with your type to learn most about yourself, but don't stop there. Each book focuses on a particular type and will be valuable for that type, but will be equally valuable for family, friends, bosses, and colleagues of that type.

Even before writing these books, I found myself doing extensive reading on the types of my brother, parents, friends, and even dates. In my business, I would research the types of my assistants, employees, and potential business partners. I found that learning about myself got me 60% of the way, and the other 40% came from learning about the other people in my life.

If you plan to read up on all the different types, I suggest looking at my "Collection" books, which include four books on four types as part of a collection, for a reduced price. This will be easier and a better price for you than buying each individual book.

You'll find a link to all the other books in this series at the end of this book.

# ADVICE FROM ENFPS FOR ENFPS

After publishing the first edition of this book, I reached out to a group of ENFPs. I asked them what advice they would share with a younger, perhaps less experienced ENFP that would help them live the best life possible.

I thought I would include them in this updated edition, and what better place than here.

You can learn a lot about a type by what they say, and also by how they say it. For this reason, I have made minimal edits to the advice shared here.

*"Try and master something you truly love at an early age."*

*"Listen to your gut; it's nearly always right."*

*"Wise and learned am I in the ways of the ENFP...*

*And from my infinite font of wisdom I do conjure the timeless advice...*

*Party hard."*

*"It's fine to want and have a career, but make sure you remember who you are and don't sacrifice that - although you could make short-term gains eventually you will regret it. Stay true to your ENFPness."*

*"We are rare, so don't be surprised if you feel as you are alien from some other planet (and I don't mean this Venus vs Mars stuff)."*

*"The earlier you learn to accept that your tendency to see and experience things differently doesn't necessarily mean you're wrong, the better off you'll be. Trust that you have a valid and helpful point of view, even if it's one that others may not understand at times."*

*"Be who you are, even if it's scary to be so different from what you think you "should" be/do/want. I spent years trying to shove myself into an ESFJ mold (like my dad) with business school (instead of psych, sociology, etc.), and working toward material goods instead of figuring out what I really wanted. What a waste of time."*

*"You have one life. Live it like you mean it and remember at the end of the line, it's YOU that has to live with the decisions you make. Be that person you want to be proud of. A wise friend once told me, own your mistakes, you can't learn from them if you don't accept they are yours. I've learnt that the mistakes I have made helped shape me into this pretty awesome person I am today. Learn to forgive yourself and let go, and you can't change someone that doesn't want to change themselves."*

*"You know what you're doing now? Keep doing it."*

*"Exploring the unknown can yield one of three results: failure, from which one can learn; success, from which one can revel - and death, from which one can never recover.*

*Have no fear to explore the unknown: the results can only ever be positive."*

This section of the book will always be growing. If you're an "experienced" ENFP and you'd like to add your insight, wisdom, and advice to upcoming editions, you can email me at: me@thedanjohnston.com.

# INTRODUCTION TO MYERS-BRIGGS®

I first officially discovered personality psychology about five years ago. I say officially because I do have some vague memories of taking a career test in high school that was likely based on the Myers-Briggs® instrument, but who really pays attention to tests when you are 16?

The Myers-Briggs assessment is one of many options in the world of personality profiles and testing. It is arguably the most popular, and in my opinion it is the best place to start. I say this because the results provide insight into all aspects of our lives, whereas other tests are often focused on just career.

The Myers-Briggs instrument is based on the idea that people are quite different from one another. These differences go deeper than emotions, moods, or environment, and speak to how we're actually wired to behave.

And, as it turns out, most people end up being wired 1 of 16 ways, based on four groups of characteristics.

This doesn't mean we can't build certain traits or change our behavior. Rather, knowing your personality type is an opportunity to learn which traits come most naturally to you and which areas you may find challenging or need to invest time in developing.

Your type provides a platform to understand yourself and create a plan for personal growth based on your unique personality strengths and weaknesses.

It is also an opportunity to understand the people around you and get to the root of many conflicts. In fact, you may find that understanding the different types and how others relate to you is the most valuable aspect of the Myers-Briggs instrument.

# THE 16 TYPES AND 4 GROUPS

Myers-Briggs assessment includes 16 different personality types that are described by a unique series of four letters.

At first, the types appear confusing, but they're really quite simple.

Each type is based on one of two modes of being or thinking for each of the four letters.

E (extrovert) or I (introvert)

N (intuitive) or S (sensing)

T (thinking) or F (feeling)

P (perceiving) or J (judging)

Now, don't pay too much attention to the words tied to each letter because they don't actually offer a great description for the characteristic.

In just a second, I'll share my explanation for each letter. But just before this, I want to share an important point to remember: Personality analysis and profiling is a bit of an art, as well as a science. In other words, since people are so diverse, the descriptions and results aren't always black and white. Some people have a strong preference for one mode or the other, but others are closer to the middle. It's natural for all of us occasionally to feel or demonstrate traits of the other types.

## What The Four Letters Mean

As you know, there are four letters that make up your personality type.

At first these letters can be a little confusing, especially since their descriptions aren't the most telling.

Here's how I explain each letter.

**For the first letter in your type, you are either an E or an I.**

The E or I describes how we relate with other people and social situations.

Extroverts are drawn to people, groups, and new social situations. They are generally comfortable at parties and in large groups.

Introverts are more reserved. This is not to say that Introverts do not enjoy people, they do. Introverts are just happier in smaller groups, and with people they know and trust, like friends or family. Keep in mind, this does not mean that Introverts are not capable of mastering social skills if they must. Rather, they will not be drawn to such situations or find the process as exciting or enjoyable as an Extrovert would.

"The Deal Breaker": For some people E or I is obvious. For others, the line is blurred. This question will make your preference clear: "Does being around new people or groups add to or drain your energy? If you spent an entire day alone would you feel "off" or bad, or would you be just fine?" If you can spend a day or two alone without feeling bad, or if spending a few hours in a group of people leaves you feeling tired, well then, you're an Introvert.

While Extroverts may often steal a lot of the attention in a room, Introverts often have the upper hand. While many Extroverts crave the spotlight, Introverts are able to sit back and calmly observe, learning more about a situation and making their contributions more meaningful and impactful.

On the other hand, Extroverts have many advantages when it comes to first impressions, wide social circles, and the ability to have fun in large groups and make new friends.

ENFPs are Extroverts. This is why ENFPs can get so much joy (and energy) from other people.

## For the second letter, you are either an N or an S.

This trait describes how you interact with the world.

Those with the intuitive trait (N) tend to be introspective and imaginative. They enjoy theoretical discussions and "big picture" kind of ideas. For an extreme example, imagine a philosophy professor with a stained suit jacket and a terribly messy office.

Of course, this isn't the reality for most N's. Most intuitive people live a happy, fulfilled life full of new ideas and inspirations...all while managing the day-to-day aspects of their lives at an acceptable level. N's have an exceptional imagination and ability to form new ideas, tell stories, and inspire those around them.

Those with the sensor trait are observant and in touch with their immediate environment. They prefer practical, "hands on" information to theory. They prefer facts over ideas. For an extreme example, think of a mechanic or military strategist.

ENFPs have the intuitive trait. This is why they are creative, great problem solvers, and drawn to big ideas.

## Third, you are either a T or an F.

This trait describes how you make decisions and come to conclusions, as well as what role emotions play in your personality and how you deal with them.

Those with the thinker trait are "tough-minded." They tend to be objective and impersonal with others. This can make them appear uncaring, but they are generally very fair. Those with the thinking trait rely on logic and rational arguments for their decisions. The "T" trait would be common among (successful) investors and those who need to make impersonal and objective decisions in their careers.

Those with the feeler trait are personal, friendly, and sympathetic to others. Their decisions are often influenced by their emotions or the "people" part of a situation. They are also more sensitive, less afraid to show their emotions to the outside world, and more affected by their emotions. The "F" trait would be common among counselors and psychologists.

## Lastly, you are either a P or a J.

This trait describes how you organize information in our internal and external worlds. This translates into how you evaluate and organize ideas and options, assess what is possible, and maintain a schedule.

I've never liked the term "Perceiver." It is better to describe this type as "Probers" or "Explorers." These people look for options, opportunities, and alternatives. They tend to be creative and open-minded. They're also likely to have a really messy bedroom or office. Perceivers are happy to try out a plan before they have all the details because they know they can always make adjustments later on if they have to.

Judgers are structured and organized. They tend to be more consistent and scheduled. Spreadsheets may be their friends and their rooms will be clean... or at least organized. They prefer concrete plans and closure over openness and possibilities.

You would find more P's among artists and creative groups, whereas professions like accountants and engineers would be dominated by J's.

ENFPs have the perceiving trait. This is one reason they are not always organized, focused, or disciplined. This is also one of the reasons ENFPs are so open to new ideas and able to come up with fresh perspectives.

# THE 16 TYPES AND 4 GROUPS

## THE FOUR GROUPS

Since the original creation of the 16 personality types, psychologists have recognized four distinct groups, each containing four types. The four types within each group have distinct traits in common based on sharing two of the four traits.

- The four types are:
- The Artisans (The SPs)
- The Guardians (The SJs)
- The Idealists (The NFs)
- The Rationals (The NTs)

**As an ENFP, you are an Idealist.**

Idealists are abstract and compassionate. Seeking meaning and significance, they are concerned with personal growth and finding their own unique identity. Their greatest strength is diplomacy. They excel at clarifying, individualizing, unifying, and inspiring.

The other three Idealist types are:

- The Leaders: ENFJs
- The Protectors: INFJs
- The Prince and Princesses: INFPs

To learn more about how all the types relate and interact, download the free compatibility chart at:

> http://www.personalitytypestraining.com/thrive/

# ENFP'S FOUR FUNCTIONS

It is important for you to know what the ENFP's four functions are, even if you don't know the science behind them. For starters, all types have the same four functions: intuition, sensing, thinking, and feeling. The differences are in how the individual uses the function (introverted vs extroverted), and the order in which the functions serve as strengths.

This will all make more sense as you read this book and continue your studies.

This will all make more sense as you read this book and continue your studies.

If it helps to get you started, here is my best attempt to explain the four functions in human terms. Many online resources use confusing technical language and psych speak when explaining this. I'll try to do the opposite here.

Think of the four functions as your four potential superpowers. Like an RPG videogame, your starting character has certain potential abilities you can gain access to as you grow. If you select the Elf, you will have access to different powers than the Orc or the Knight.

### The eight available functions are:

- Extroverted Intuition (Ne)
- Introverted Intuition (Ni)
- Extroverted Sensing (Se)
- Introverted Sensing (Si)
- Extroverted Feeling (Fe)
- Introverted Feeling (Fi)

- Extroverted Thinking (Te)
- Introverted Thinking (Ti)

Note that the E or I attached to each function is not an indicator of the individual's preference to introversion or extroversion. Rather, it is an indicator of how they use the particular function.

Which four functions a type has, and the order in which they are strengths, is determined by the types preferences on the Extroversion vs Introversion, and Perceiving vs Judging measures. I'm going to leave it there, as any explanation beyond this would give us both a psychology jargon headache.

In your early years, your personality is ruled by your dominant function. This shapes your early strengths as well as weaknesses. Over time, through challenge and experience, you develop your second (auxiliary) and third (tertiary) "functions." You create a more powerful and balanced personality. You minimize weak spots, mature emotionally, and develop a diverse set of skills.

## The key to overcoming most personality challenges is developing (strengthening) the weaker functions.

In general, we grow our primary (or dominant) function in our early years, our secondary function in our twenties and thirties, and our third function some time in our thirties and forties. However, this pattern assumes you're not being proactive or reading a book like this one. In your case, there is no reason you can't leap ahead a few decades and strengthen your other functions ahead of schedule. Actually, doing so is essential to your personal development.

## How We Use Our Functions

In the following section, you will notice each function is described as either introverted or extroverted. This is an indicator of use.

For example, an INFJ has "introverted intuition." This means they use their intuition to internally process ideas and situations and come to conclusions. Their secondary function is "extroverted feeling." This means they interact with the outside world using their feeling function. It also means most inputs are filed through the INFJ's feeling function before reaching their intuition.

An ENFP has "extroverted intuition" as their dominant function. This means the ENFP interacts with and experiences the outside world using their intuition. For an ENFP, their secondary function is "introverted feeling." This means the ENFP processes their thoughts and judgments internally based on their feelings.

### An ENFP has the following functions:

**Dominant Function - Extroverted Intuition (Ne):** This is how the ENFP interacts and understands the outside world. Ne is about hidden meaning, alternatives, and possibilities. This function powers the ENFP's ability to create new ideas and a unique vision for the future. Their vision can then become a catalyst for action.

**Auxiliary Function - Introverted Feeling (Fi):** This is the ENFP's second strongest function and is used to interpret and judge the outside world against an internal set of values built around harmony and authenticity. This function gives the ENFP an ability to read between the lines and sense what is false or inauthentic in a situation.

**Tertiary Function - Extroverted Thinking (Te):** This is the

ENFP's third function. Te strives to be efficient and productive through organization and scheduling. Te is all about logic, seeking the root cause for an action, as well as spotting faulty reasoning.

It should come as no surprise that developing their thinking function will help the ENFP become more organized and disciplined. It will also support them in handling confrontational situations. Exactly how to do this is addressed more in the Overcoming Your Weaknesses section, as well as in other areas of this book.

**Inferior Function - Introverted Sensing (Se):** This is the least developed of the ENFP's functions. ENFPs are future oriented, rarely looking over their shoulder at either the successes or disasters left in their wake. Se provides them often needed connection to the past.

## CONNECTING WITH THE PAST

As an ENFP myself, I'm all too familiar with the fast pace and occasional chaos that can accompany our lives. Yes, this is where ENFPs thrive. We love change and challenge, and have no problem with uncertainty or risk. Yet, this state of being can wear on us.

One way for us ENFPs to develop our Se is to take a half an hour or so a few times a month to live in the past. Not only does this develop our Se, it also provides a calming feeling and a temporary escape from the present.

Now, the key here is to complete an activity that you've done many times, providing an easy connection to the past. You should not be challenged here! Some ways to do this include building something with for example a Lego set or doing puzzle you've done many times before, creating a sculpture or doing painting, listening to the same CD, or watching a favorite show.

Ideally, the best activities involve some kind of physical activity as well, such as the building ones. With that said, one of my favorites is to re-watch the "Vegas Baby Vegas" episode of Entourage. I must have watched it 50 times now.

# DISCOVERING THE CHAMPION: WHO IS AN ENFP?

At this point, I'm going to assume you're an ENFP and are reading about yourself, or reading about someone you care about who is an ENFP.

I'm also going to assume you've read some of the basic descriptions online about ENFPs and have bought this book because you want depth and details on how ENFPs can thrive.

So with that, I won't bore you with a drawn out description of ENFPs. I'll keep it short and let you get on to the other chapters where we go deeper into specific areas like career and relationships.

ENFPs delight in movement and are often the catalyst for change on a societal level. While they are often bored with the details and may struggle to "follow through" on plans, ENFPs have an incredible ability to initiate change and get the ball rolling. This stems from a combination of three ENFP abilities:

1 - ENFPs are able to develop a unique, uncompromised, and inspiring vision for the future.

2 - ENFPs have a dislike for the established: be it rules, ways of doing things, or authority. This inspires them (and others) if they choose to take on an established organization or way of thinking, and provides them with an almost unlimited source of energy.

3 - An ENFP's enthusiasm, charisma, and inspiring vision for the future act as a natural magnet and attracts people to their cause. An ENFP on a mission will soon find themselves surrounded by dozens, if not hundreds or thousands of people willing to put it all on the line to help the ENFP achieve their

vision.

In all they do, ENFPs bring a liveliness and sense of play to life. This makes them fun co-workers, friends, and partners. When they focus on their strengths, ENFPs excel. When they move outside their strengths, ENFPs can still find a marginal level of success, but will not be as happy or perform at their best.

One challenge for the ENFP is that they can be "good" at many things because they are naturally intelligent, they're quick learners, and are very adaptable. This leads many ENFPs down a path of mediocrity. ENFPs must not settle for good and instead should seek opportunities to use their true strengths and become great.

Another common scenario for ENFPs is the search for their purpose or the sweet spot where they really do excel. This is a good path for the ENFP, but can appear to be unfocused to the outside world. In the Kryptonite chapter we talk about this "Shiny Objects Syndrome" and how to overcome it.

Overall, ENFPs are fun, optimistic, and caring individuals who want the best for themselves and the people around them. When they discover themselves and focus on their true purpose, an ENFP is capable of tremendous levels of success and of making a positive impact on the world.

# IN GOOD COMPANY: FAMOUS ENFPS

As an ENFP, you are among some very good company. In this chapter you'll find a collection of famous and "successful" people who are either confirmed, or suspected, as being ENFPs.

Do not use this chapter as a guide to what you must do or whom you must resemble. Rather, use this chapter as a source of inspiration. It is a chance to see what's possible as an ENFP and what great things have been accomplished by those who share a similar makeup to you.

Personally, I have found great value studying famous people from my own type through autobiographies. Most of us spend the early years of our lives feeling lost and trying to figure out our purpose or how we want to end up. I've found studying those of my type who have found their purpose, and have then achieved success, gives me a shortcut to understanding my own potential and the directions my life could go.

## Famous ENFPs

### Writers, Creators, and Thought Leaders

- Mark Twain
- Hunter S. Thompson
- Oscar Wilde
- Aldous Huxley
- Umberto Eco
- Salman Rushdie
- Julian Assange
- Ralph Nader
- Anne Frank
- Arianna Huffington
- Walt Disney

- Kurt Vonnegut
- Osho
- Naomi Klein
- Michio Kaku (Physicist)
- Brian Cox (Physicist)
- Joseph Campbell
- Alan Watts
- Jacques Derrida

## Actors and Performers

- Robin Williams
- Jerry Seinfeld
- Gwen Stefani
- Ellen Degeneres
- Keira Knightley
- Katie Couric
- Orson Welles
- Oliver Stone
- George Carlin
- Jack White
- Sarah Michelle Gellar
- Sharon Stone
- Sandra Bullock
- Alicia Silverstone
- Daniel Radcliffe

## Politicians

- Ralph Nader
- Che Guevara
- Fidel Castro
- Muammar Gaddafi
- Hugo Chavez

*Worth Noting:* If you haven't yet read up on any of the other types, you may not notice the distinctions of the famous ENFPs. Compared with other types, there is a heavy weighting towards writing, outside the box philosophy, and performing.

In the political arena, ENFPs aren't interested in run of the mill politics. ENFPs only get involved when they're trying to right an injustice or make a massive change in the way things are done.

## Going Deeper Exercise

Of the famous ENFPs on this list, which are most familiar to you?

_____
_____
_____
_____
_____

What are some common elements you notice? These could be specific personality traits or characteristics. It could also include actions they have taken or tough decisions they have made. For example: going against the grain or choosing to follow a passion.

_____
_____
_____
_____
_____

# YOUR SECRET WEAPONS

### (Aka your unique strengths)

In my own life, I have found no greater success secret than discovering, *and applying*, my strengths.

If a student is gifted in math but struggles in English, she may not be accepted to any university because her average grade would be too low. The whole system teaches one to be "well rounded."

Yet, the real world doesn't reward the well-rounded individual, at least not exceptionally well. Those who receive the greatest rewards are those who focus on their strengths and ignore all else. Think of people like Arnold Schwarzenegger, Steve Jobs, and Oprah Winfrey.

Does anyone *really* care if Oprah is bad at math, if Arnold has trouble managing his personal life, or if Steve Jobs was a bit of an ass to employees from time to time?

Nope. No one cares because each of these Greats focused on their strengths and created an extraordinary life for themselves.

Oprah (an ENFJ) harnessed her empathy and ability to build trust and bond with people to create incredible interviews and connect with her audience.

Arnold (an INTJ) used his focus, discipline, and strategic thinking to achieve incredible goals in fitness, performing, and politics, despite being the underdog in most everything he ever did.

Steve Jobs (an ISTP) kept his energy focused on his creative and visual strengths. His visions were so clear, and his innovations so impressive, that his social graces didn't matter.

Now, as you read on, you will discover the unique strengths

closely linked to ENFPs. While you read this, remember that these are the strengths that come naturally to you, but you still need to develop and fine-tune them if you want to thrive.

ENFPs' strengths tend to revolve around their ability to quickly absorb and process information, spot patterns, connect with people, be themselves (authenticity), and communicate in an effective and inspiring way.

## An ENFP's Secret Weapons

- ENFPs are "quick." They're able to quickly assess information or situations and come to surprisingly accurate conclusions before anyone else in the room does.
- ENFPs' quickness is tied to their perceptiveness and intelligence. As part of these same abilities, they're able to see connections between people, situations, and ideas that most others miss. This often leads them to create new ideas.
- ENFPs are able to quickly connect with other people and develop rapport, making those around them feel comfortable.
- ENFPs can quickly read a room or social situation and adapt so they fit in. They are quick on their feet and can answer a question or rebut with a joke without hesitation.
- ENFPs are enthusiastic, happy, and optimistic. This is often why the type is called the "Inspirer."
- ENFPs are extremely accepting of other people and their differences. They see people are equal and tend to believe in everyone's potential.
- ENFPs are generally very creative and intelligent.
- ENFPs are able to take in lots of information, process the

important parts, and reach a decision in a quick timeframe.
- ENFPs are very adaptive and can function well in most situations. They're very comfortable with change.
- ENFPs have exceptional communication skills, both spoken and written. They're able to understand what someone is trying to say when others in the room are clueless. Similarly, they're able to communicate in a way that others can understand, almost speaking their own subtle language.
- When connected with an issue or individual, an ENFP can become a very passionate advocate. This passion gives them the ability to inspire large groups of people or create movements.

### In summary, a developed ENFP can be:

- Intelligent
- Quick
- Adaptable
- Creative
- Well Liked
- Social
- Caring
- Intuitive
- Authentic
- Supportive
- Inspiring
- Innovative

## Keys To Using Your Strengths As An ENFP:

1. Spend time with people every day.
2. Avoid being the "finisher" on projects.
3. Develop and trust your intuition; it will usually be right.

In this and future chapters you will discover "Going Deeper" exercises. These are designed to help you better understand and apply the chapter's content. If you're like me, you may want to write your answers down. When you bought this book you also got access to a companion workbook you can print and then fill in with your answers as you go. You can download the workbook for free at:

http://www.personalitytypestraining.com/thrive/

## GOING DEEPER EXERCISE

Of the strengths listed above, which most jump out at you as strengths of your own?

_____
_____
_____
_____
_____

What are three strengths listed above that you know you have but are not actively using in your life, at least not as much as you know you should?

_____
_____
_____
_____
_____

How could you apply these strengths more frequently?

_____
_____
_____
_____
_____

# YOUR KRYPTONITE

## (Aka your potential weaknesses)

You didn't think I was going to stop at your strengths, did you? As much as I say *focus on your strengths*, it is still important to be aware of your weaknesses, even if it is just so that you can ignore them more easily.

Below, you will find a list of weaknesses or challenges common among ENFPs. As with strengths, this is not a definitive list and do not take it as a prescription for how ENFPs have to be.

Sometimes I will see posts in a Facebook group for a specific type where people seem overly proud of their type challenges. I remember one post on an ENFP group making light of how the poster had been unable to tidy their room in four days. While it was good for a "we've all been there" chuckle, I did find myself turned off when I thought about what a chaotic life this person must have.

This person chose not to fix their weakness. For example, they could have chosen to develop their self-discipline and, over time, it would become easier to stay tidy. They were also unwilling to just accept this weakness and find another solution. If they decided to embrace it, then they could have just hired a maid. Instead, they chose to suffer what they described as four days of agony simply trying to clean a room.

### At The Root of an ENFP's Struggle

ENFPs' challenges tend to revolve around focus, follow through, and the details of life. ENFPs will find life easier and more fun if they learn to develop their "Thinker" trait, surround themselves with people strong in organization and follow through, and give themselves permission to outsource their weaknesses.

If some of these weaknesses don't really resonate with you, that's **good**. Do not assume you should be weak in an area simply because you read it here. It is very possible that you are wired a little differently, or that you've already developed beyond some of your inborn weak spots.

On the other hand, if you find yourself nodding in agreement while reading, take it as an opportunity to either improve that area of yourself, or accept it and find a another way to deal with it.

*Note: You'll find more on "outsourcing" your weaknesses in the later chapter Practical Problems to Common Challenges.*

### ENFPs may experience the following challenges at one time or another:

- Being gullible, or "the sucker." An ENFP who has not developed their thinking trait or worldly experience can often fall victim to believing just about everything they hear. When this happens, they become ideal targets for con men, multi-level marketers, and motivational speakers. This happens because ENFPs want to see the best in others, because of their desire to get along with others, because of their overall optimistic nature, and because of the importance authenticity plays in their own lives.
- The ENFPs' love for excitement and newness can lead them into dangerous situations. This can happen on both the practical level, such as in dark alleyways, and on larger life levels, such as in dangerous financial situations or when entering into a risky business.
- ENFPs can often struggle with personal finances. Part of this stems from their perceiving and feeling traits. It also

stems from their optimistic personalities, as well as in the frequency with which ENFPs change careers.
- ENFPs do not like to be controlled or to control others. This can lead to problems with employers, or to problems as employers themselves when their employees need more structure, direction, or discipline.
- ENFPs generally shy away from confrontation. Life is good when the people around them are happy. This may lead to avoidance behavior, rising tensions, or unresolved issues in relationships.
- ENFPs are very sensitive to negative criticism and yet can be quick to form long-lasting negative judgments of other people.
- Because they love new stimulation, ENFPs are at risk of having a little too much fun with drugs, alcohol, and sex.

## SHINY OBJECT SYNDROME

Now, there is one last thing to add to this list and it is perhaps the most dangerous kryptonite of all for the ENFP. Many ENFPs who are struggling in life are also struggling with or perhaps because of the Shiny Object Syndrome.

These ENFPs bounce from one career or relationship to the next. As soon as the newness wears off they are ready to jump ship to the next thing. When something new and "shiny" appears to them, their first instinct is to drop whatever they're doing and try it out.

Now, in their quest for the perfect job or partner, it is normal for ENFPs to change careers and relationships more than most other types. This is part of the ENFPs natural development. Yes, from the outside world, these ENFPs appear to be flakey or "all over the map." This doesn't matter, because successful ENFPs have a strong internal compass and know the direction they want to move in. Each change brings them closer to their desired outcome.

The problem comes when ENFPs become addicted to the excitement of newness and change. They enjoy the early parts of the learning curve but quit before becoming exceptional. They may also always be looking for the next big opportunity, easy money, or newest greatest thing.

These ENFPs have yet to develop their ability to think objectively, to think long term, and to find their own values and internal compass. Until they do, they will suffer from Shiny Object Syndrome. Their kryptonite may also include:

- Bouncing from relationship to relationship, never finding a deep or fulfilling connection.
- Being unable to finish projects; starting dozens, finishing none.
- Switching careers, business direction, or even relationships whenever they come up against a challenge, because they lack the discipline to follow through.
- When an ENFP becomes known for the above traits, they may lose the respect of those around them. They may also lose their ability to inspire others with their grand visions once it is recognized that the ENFP's vision changes every week and never seems to turn into anything real.

## Overcoming Your Weaknesses

The keys to success as an ENFP revolve around developing your thinking function. This is your ability to be objective, rational, and disciplined. Your Te function will also help you stay focused and organized, and keep you moving in a focused direction. As you develop your Te, you will learn to develop longer time frames for your goals, and therefore be more likely to overcome obstacles and follow through.

**Here are a few more ways you can develop your Te:**

- Take time to study those who have succeeded and pay attention to how much time they invested into their success before they saw results.
- Learn to be just a little "realistic"... even if that is a forbidden word for most ENFPs.
- Spent more time with Rationals (those with the NT traits) and observe how they think and make decisions.
- Stop reading new-age and self-help books that proclaim you can have it all without hard work or sacrifice. Those authors are lying to you just so that they can steal your money. A perfect example of this is the law of attraction (in its mainstream movie-modified, just sit on the sofa and wish for a new house, kind of way).

You'll find more on this topic in the later section, Keys To Health, Happiness, and Success.

## GOING DEEPER EXERCISE

Of the weaknesses listed above, which three do you most recognize in yourself?

_____
_____
_____
_____
_____

What are three weaknesses listed above that you know are having a significant negative impact on your success?

_____
_____
_____
_____
_____

How could you reduce the impact these weaknesses have on your life, either by learning to overcome them or eliminating the activities that bring them to the surface?

_____
_____
_____
_____
_____

# IDEAL CAREER OPTIONS FOR AN ENFP

If you gave a Myers-Briggs test to a group of a few hundred people from the same profession, you would see a very clear pattern.

An accountant in my martial arts class told me that of 600 chartered accountants who took the Myers-Briggs test at his firm, he was one of only three people who didn't score the same type.

This happens for two reasons:

1) Selection Bias: People with the personality type for accounting will tend to do well in related tasks and receive hints that that kind of work is right for them. They may especially enjoy numbers, spreadsheets, etc.
2) Survival Bias: Those with the personality type for accounting are most likely to pass the vigorous tests and internships required to become a charted accountant.

We are actually much better at finding our path than we give ourselves credit for. In almost every profession, there is a significantly higher percentage of those "typed" to excel in it than random chance would allow.

Yet, many people still slip through the cracks, or spend decades searching for their perfect career before finding it.

This chapter will help you avoid the cracks and stop wasting your precious time. Below, you'll find a comprehensive list of careers ENFPs tend to be drawn to and succeed in.

There are many ENFP career options included on websites and guides that I have intentionally excluded here.

These include "good" career options in which an ENFP could easily succeed but would be unlikely to find real happiness or fulfillment. This list focuses on careers where an ENFP can focus on their strengths.

I have included only the options I believe ENFPs have an upper hand in *and* those in which there is the highest likelihood to find fulfillment and success. There are always other options, but why swim upstream if you don't need to, right?

**To be most successful, an ENFP should focus on work that:**

- Allows them to follow their inspirations and create new products, ideas, or ways of doing things.
- Rewards enthusiasm, imagination, original thought, and ideas.
- Is aligned with their personal beliefs and values. To an ENFP, authenticity is very important, and they must believe in the work they are doing.
- Includes a variety of people, projects, and challenges, so the day is filled with fun and excitement.
- Allows them to be the "Starter" on projects and does not force them to handle the details or finish the work they get started.
- Happens within a friendly and supportive environment with a minimal amount of conflict.

## Popular Professions For ENFPs

### In Creative Fields

- Journalist
- Screenwriter
- Playwright
- Documentary filmmaker
- Character actor
- Reporter/editor (magazine)
- Columnist
- Newscaster
- Interior decorator
- Musician/composer
- Artist
- Desktop publisher
- Art director
- Creative director on a multimedia team
- Developer of educational software
- Multimedia producer
- Theatre director
- Television producer
- Costume/wardrobe designer
- Broadcast news analyst
- Cartoonist and animator
- Exhibit designer

### Corporate/Technology

- Customer relations manager
- Staff advocate
- Project manager
- Engagement manager
- Human resources recruiter

### Marketing/Planning

- Public relations specialist
- Marketing consultant
- Advertising account executive
- Copywriter
- Advertising creative director
- Strategic planner
- Publicist
- Research assistant
- Editor/art director

### Education/Counseling

- Special education teacher
- Bilingual education teacher
- Early childhood education teacher
- Teacher: art/drama/ music/English
- Child welfare counselor
- Substance abuse counselor
- Social worker
- Development director
- Career counselor
- Ombudsperson
- Pastoral counselor
- Rehabilitation worker
- Social scientist
- Educational psychologist
- Social psychologist
- Counseling psychologist
- Anthropologist
- Philanthropic consultant
- High school guidance counselor

## Health Care and Social Service

- Dietitian or nutritionist
- Speech-language pathologist/audiologist
- Holistic health practitioner
- Massage therapist
- Employee assistance program counselor
- Legal mediator
- Urban regional planner
- Public health educator

## Entrepreneurial or Business Pursuits

- Consultant
- Business/Life Coach
- Inventor
- Sales: Selling intangibles (ideas)
- Human resources manager
- Conference planner
- Restaurateur
- Merchandise planner
- Personnel recruiter
- Labor relations specialist
- PR specialist
- Marketing executive for TV, Radio, Digital Media

## Going Deeper Exercise

After reading through the list of careers, answer the following questions:

Which 5-10 careers jump out at you as something you'd enjoy doing?

_____
_____
_____
_____
_____

Thinking back to the sections on strengths, what do you notice about the list of careers? What strengths might contribute to success in these careers?

_____
_____
_____
_____
_____

Is your current career or career path on the list? If it isn't, how does it stack up against the list of workplace criteria? Could it still be an environment in which you find success?

_____
_____
_____
_____
_____

# THRIVING AT WORK

There is an astronomical difference between a job you're good at and a career you love and in which you thrive.

While some people are fine just getting by, people like you and I sure aren't. This section will help you thrive at work.

## THREE FOUNDATIONS FOR THRIVING AT WORK

1) Be aware of your strengths and weaknesses and be selective of the work you do. Be honest in job interviews about where you excel as well as where you struggle.

2) When in a job, take this same honest approach with your supervisor. Explain that you aren't being lazy; rather you feel you could deliver much more *value* to the company by focusing on your strengths.

3) At least once per week, if not daily, stop for a few minutes and ask yourself: "Am I working in my strengths or struggling in my weaknesses?"

Remember, you have unique and valuable gifts. Make the effort to use them and avoid getting trapped in the wrong kind of work.

**When it comes to your work, be sure to tap into these work related strengths for ENFPs:**

- The ability to think outside the box and find new possibilities.
- Excellent communication abilities and the ability to engage others and activate their enthusiasm for an idea or project.

- The ability to easily understand others. ENFPs can often "read between the lines." Where others miss an unspoken point, ENFPs are able to grasp the true meaning of the spoken message.
- Adaptability. ENFPs can quickly change direction, often without skipping a beat. This makes them great "go-to" people who can be counted on to get the job done.
- The ability to see the big picture and use this knowledge to predict the consequences of certain actions or ideas.
- ENFPs are independent and able to jump into a project, take risks, and do whatever is needed without much supervision or guidance.
- ENFPs usually have a broad range of interests and the ability to learn a new skill or area of business quite quickly.

**To maximize their success, ENFPs should be aware of some challenges they face at work. ENFPs will not always, but may:**

- Be disorganized or unscheduled.
- Have trouble prioritizing tasks or planning their work and therefore can be indecisive as to what to do next.
- Be impatient with those who are less creative than them, or those who tend to "ponder" things before making a decision.
- Become bored or sidetracked when the exciting part of a project ends or when confronted by repetitive tasks. They may lack the discipline to complete tasks or follow through on details. This becomes a problem when the ENFP is responsible for these details, and hence why it is essential for ENFPs to find a career that supports their strengths.
- Dislike rigid tasks, people, or systems. This means a strict corporate environment is literally the living embodiment

of hell for an ENFP.
- Be unrealistic and put too much focus on what "could be possible" and then come up short of their objectives.
- Dislike criticism and conflict. This can lead to trouble receiving feedback from superiors, or giving it to subordinates.
- Be weak at estimating how long things will take. Being idealists, they tend to assume things will happen much quicker than they actually do. This can lead to missing deadlines or being forced to work weekends. It is also one reason many ENFPs are always running a little late.

## Going Deeper Exercise

Have any of the strengths or weaknesses listed in this chapter been brought to your attention by a boss or colleague before?

___

Which of the strengths did you instantly recognize in yourself? Are they any you've been underutilizing in your current career?

___

Which one or two weaknesses, if you were to totally overcome them, would have the greatest positive impact on your career?

___

# RICH AND HAPPY RELATIONSHIPS

Whoever said opposites attract never met an ENFP + ISTJ couple.

Sure, you want a partner who complements your strengths and weaknesses, but most of us also want someone who understands us – someone to whom we can express our opinions and ideas and be understood.

In this section, we'll start with a discussion on what ENFPs are like in relationships. Then, we'll look at the most common personality types ENFPs are happy with. Lastly, we will provide some advice on creating and maintaining successful relationships as an ENFP and *with* an ENFP.

## ENFPs In Relationships

ENFPs tend to be fun, loving, exciting, and loyal partners. They are generally disinterested in the day-to-day maintenance of their relationship or home and are more focused on moments of passion and their creative inspirations.

The partner of an ENFP can expect surprises ranging from luxurious gifts and vacations to periods of frugality.

ENFPs are generally drawn to novelty. An immature ENFP may find themselves bouncing from one short relationship to another without ever developing anything real. A developed ENFP will learn to fulfill their need for novelty and excitement through other mediums, such as vacations or sports, as well as by learning to discover deeper levels of themselves and their partner.

## ENFPs' Ideal Matches

A note on compatibility: There is no be all and end all. The information on type compatibility is either based on theory or surveys, neither of which will ever provide a universal rule.

For example, according to surveys, NF (idealist) types find the greatest relationship *satisfaction* dating other NFs. So for the ENFP, this means dating INFJs, ENFJs, INFPs, and possibly other ENFPs. This satisfaction is likely because Idealists share a common way of thinking and feeling about the world.

Yet according to Jung, the ideal partner for an ENFP is an INTJ. The two have very complementary personalities and are perhaps most likely to be successful in a business partnership or in creating a home... but this doesn't mean they will find true love together.

Don't take these suggestions as limits to who you can be with. Ultimately, the two individuals, and their desire to grow and work to create an incredible relationship, will be the biggest determination of their success together.

With that said, one incompatibility I've noticed time and time again is between Intuitives (N) and Sensors (S). I think this is because these two groups have fundamentally different ways of interacting with the world and often have trouble understanding one another.

In my own experience in romantic relationships, friendships, and business partnerships, I (a strong Intuitive - ENFP), have always run into trouble with strong Sensors.

Beyond that caveat, it's all up in the air. Generally, for organization sake, I would suggest that P's match with a J. The P will benefit from the J's structure and organization, and the J will benefit from the P's creativity and spontaneity.

## Tips For Dating As An ENFP

1. Stop trying to please people and learn to value your own needs as well. Don't adjust your actions or opinions to gain approval or conform to groups. This behavior may help your dating life in the short term, but in the long run it will sabotage your ability to find a mate you're truly compatible with.

2. Avoid dating Sensors. In the short term they will be drawn to your creativity, spontaneity, and all round fun attitude, but you will never be able to communicate with one another on a higher level.

3. ENFPs can be overly enthusiastic. In the early stages of a relationship, avoid making gushy or smothering comments during the moments you just happen to feel something strong.
   You may turn some partners off, and you may give other partners unrealistic expectations about how strongly you feel for them.

4. ENFPs have a strong dislike of conflict, criticism, and confrontation. You will benefit from developing your ability to handle conflict. The only way to do this is with baby steps, one awkward conversation at a time. You can learn more about this in the sections on developing your Te function.

5. You may set very high expectations for yourself and your partner. Just remember: Everyone is human, and no partner or relationship will be perfect. Don't be too hard on your partner or yourself.

6. If you're after a "perfect" relationship, take time to check in with your partner on this. Does he or she share your same high expectations and willingness to work at the relationship? If so, is their vision of a "perfect" relationship the same as yours? Communication around your goals and desires is essential to avoid conflict and disappointment.

7. Take time to study successful relationships. ENFPs tend to buy into the idea of fairy tale romance and the existence of a perfect relationship. While romantic, this isn't always the most realistic view. Long term relationships often take work, compromise, and personal development to succeed.

On a positive note, this belief encourages some ENFPs to work hard at creating a great relationship. On a negative note, some ENFPs may be too quick to jump ship when challenges arise. This stems from the fairy tale idea that "if we are perfect for each other then we wouldn't have any problems or challenges."

## Tips For Dating An ENFP

ENFPs are affectionate, lively, caring, and fun partners. Although they love novelty and can "date around," their desire to be authentic means if they commit to a relationship they mean it and will be loving and loyal. If you learn to work with their weaknesses, you may find yourself in a very happy and fulfilling relationship.

1. If you find yourself dating an immature ENFP, be prepared for a fun and laughter-filled relationship... and not much else.

2. ENFPs are highly intuitive and will see through most lies and artificial (i.e., fake) behavior. If you're dishonest or inauthentic they will know and you'll lose their respect.

3. In some areas ENFPs are excellent communicators, but they dislike conflict, criticism, and confrontation. This means they are uncomfortable and often unpracticed with certain kinds of discussions. As their partner, you need to be aware of this and may need to be the one to initiate uncomfortable or difficult conversations. They may initially be hesitant to put their emotions on the table, but you can encourage them by using an open and non-judgmental tone.

4. ENFPs are fun, spontaneous, and adventurous. Fighting this instinct will only cause you problems. Your best option is to embrace and enjoy it. Remember, being playful or funny is not a sign of immaturity. The ability to balance serious pursuits with a childlike playfulness is a sign of wisdom.

5. ENFPs are not organized, keen on schedules, or otherwise interested in repetitive or mundane work. If you want to build a life with an ENFP, you must accept this and accept them. Develop systems, hire help, or take responsibility for the details of your life together.

It's important to remember that we don't choose our personality traits. Yes, ENFPs can develop their Te and become better organized, but it will never be as easy for them as it is for many other types. Because of this, it is not wise to judge their effort or desire by their results. Remember the story from the kryptonite chapter about the ENFP who cowered for four days trying to clean his room.

6. ENFPs can be overly enthusiastic, so when they express their feelings for you always take it with a grain of salt. Judge them more by their actions than their words. This is especially important in the early stages of a relationship.

To learn more about how all the types relate and interact, download the free compatibility chart at:

http://www.personalitytypestraining.com/thrive/

# KEYS TO WEALTH, HEALTH, HAPPINESS, AND SUCCESS

I hope this book has provided some insights into how you can succeed in the most important areas of your life.

In this last section, I'd like to share eleven strategies for finding all around success. These strategies will help you enjoy more wealth, health, and happiness in your life.

1. ENFPs must follow their passions and do work they love. When interested in something, ENFPs have an unrivaled energy and enthusiasm. When stuck doing work they don't enjoy, ENFPs are masters of procrastination and excuses.

2. ENFPs really dislike repetitive work, so stick to "project based" work, such as launching a new marketing campaign, expanding into new territory, or creating a new product. Within this world, try and focus on the starting aspects of the project. ENFPs have an incredible ability to get things started and build momentum. This is a tremendous asset... if those things eventually get completed as well. Partner with people who enjoy the details, including putting the finishing touches on things.

3. Look out for your own needs. Your concern for those around you is a wonderful trait but there will come times where you must step aside and take care of yourself. Sometimes this will mean letting others down, that's OK. People will understand.

4. Develop your "Thinking" quality (Te). Make a conscious effort to understand and become aware of your emotions

and apply logic to your decision-making. This will allow you to become more objective and disciplined. One way to do this is to learn from the NTs in your life, particularly INTJs and ENTJs.

5. Take time to compare your initial dreams, goals, or visions with what actually did happen. This will help develop your Te as well as your goal setting and planning abilities.

   ENFPs have a wonderfully optimistic outlook on life. Unfortunately, they also excel at setting "pie in the sky" goals with unrealistic timeframes, which can lead to never actually achieving anything. Developing an accurate perception of how long things really take will help you set and achieve goals and make real progress.

6. On the note of perception, ENFPs can sometimes be too hard on other people, and have unrealistic expectations for what relationships should be like. Fuelled by movies and Usher songs, ENFPs can be quick to skip town the moment their partner reveals a flaw or when a challenge presents itself in the relationship. ENFPs will be well served to sit back and objectively look at themselves. Perhaps she will discover she isn't perfect either. You may want to enroll a friend or former partner for help in this process.

7. Plan and schedule time to be around people. ENFPs are the only extroverted type that love people but also need time alone. Unfortunately, sometimes ENFPs can fall into a negative cycle and spend too much time alone. This risk is most present for self-employed or stay-at-

home ENFPs. When alone for too long, ENFPs can lose their energy, creativity, and zest for life.

8. ENFPs have a distain for confrontation, conflict, and being told what to do. In the real world, there will be times when you need to follow orders or engage in confrontation.

   When this happens and negative emotions come up, take a moment to understand and process them. You may think to yourself: "I'm feeling upset and I think it is because I am being told what to do."

   Then, think through the situation and take the most productive and mature action that you can.

9. Face your fears to overcome your weaknesses. Learn to express your opinions in the face of criticism. Learn to be decisive. Learn to be comfortable with confrontation.

   You will only learn by doing. This means taking action and risking failure. At first, this may be very uncomfortable, but over time you will develop your abilities and it will get easier and easier.

10. Learn to understand others. You have a unique and wonderful way of looking at the world... but it is your own perspective and may not always be right for other people. Learn to understand how other people see the world and your influence will increase while the amount of conflict in your world decreases.

11. Be accountable and take personal responsibility for your actions and circumstances.

It is important to be aware of your weaknesses, but do not use this knowledge as an excuse.

Never blame others or outside forces for your situation or results. When you blame other people for your circumstances, you give away the power to change them. When you take responsibility for your life, you give yourself the power to change it.

## Practical Solutions To Common Challenges

There is an old-fashioned attitude that tells us to just tough it up, overcome our weaknesses, and do everything ourselves.

This is stupid.

If you're an exceptional painter you should spend your time painting and leave the toilet cleaning to someone else.

The more you allow yourself to offload the tasks and responsibilities you don't enjoy, the more success you will experience. Here are a few practical ideas for making the most of your strengths while avoiding your weaknesses.

### Hire Help With:

- Accounting
- Cleaning
- Laundry
- Planning travel
- Organization
- Scheduling
- Life planning (such as a coach)
- Business planning

# NEXT STEPS

To help you get the most from this book, I have created a collection of free extras to support you along the way. If you haven't already done so, take a few minutes now to request the free bonuses; you already paid for them when you bought this book. To download these, simply visit the special section of my website: www.PersonalityTypesTraining.com/thrive

There, you will be asked to enter your email address so I can send you the "Thriving Bonus Pack." You'll receive:

- A 5-part mini-course (delivered via email) with tips on how to adjust your life so that you can best make use of your strengths.
- A compatibility chart showing how you are most likely to relate to the other 15 personality types. You'll discover which types are most compatible with you and which types will likely lead to headaches.
- A PDF workbook that complements this book. It's formatted to be printed, so you can fill in your answers to the exercises in each chapter as you go.

To download the Thriving Bonus Pack, visit:

www.PersonalityTypesTraining.com/thrive

# SUGGESTIONS AND FEEDBACK

Like the field of psychology, this book will always be growing and improving.

If there's something about this book you didn't like, or there is a point you disagreed with, I'd love to hear from you. Perhaps I missed something in my research.

As well, if you're an "experienced" ENFP and you'd like to add your personal story, insight, wisdom, or advice to upcoming editions, my readers and I would love to hear from you.

To contribute in any way, you can email me at: me@thedanjohnston.com.

# A SMALL FAVOR

If you've enjoyed this book or found it useful, I'd be very grateful if you'd post a short review on Amazon. Your support really does make a difference, and I read all the reviews personally so I can get your feedback and make this book even better.

If you'd like to leave a review, then all you need to do is visit this book's page on Amazon.

Thanks again for your support!

# OTHER BOOKS ON ENFPS' AND ENFPS' BEST MATCHES: INTJS AND INFJS

### ENFP: Inspired and Inspiring

Or just visit Amazon and search for "ENFP". Then look for the book by Dan Johnston

### INFJ: The Protector and Most Disciplined of Idealists

Or just visit Amazon and search for "INFJ". Then look for the book by Dan Johnston.

### INTJ: The Persistent and Strategic Mastermind

Or just visit Amazon and search for "INTJ". Then look for the book by Dan Johnston.

### INFJ Words of Wisdom

Or just visit Amazon and search for "INFJ". Then look for the book by Dan Johnston.

### INTJ: Lessons From The Unstoppable Mastermind

Or just visit Amazon and search for "INTJ". Then look for the book by Dan Johnston..

# BOOKS IN THE THRIVE PERSONALITY TYPE SERIES

**INFP: The Prince or Princess**

Or just visit Amazon and search for "INFP". Then look for the book by Dan Johnston.

**ENFJ: The Leader, Teacher, and People Person**

Or just visit Amazon and search for "ENFJ". Then look for the book by Dan Johnston.

### ENTJ: The Unstoppable Fieldmarshal and Executive

Or just visit Amazon and search for "ENTJ". Then look for the book by Dan Johnston.

### ENTP: The Charming and Visionary Inventor

Or just visit Amazon and search for "ENTP". Then look for the book by Dan Johnston.

### INTP: The Often Genius Thinker and Architect

Or just visit Amazon and search for "INTP". Then look for the book by Dan Johnston.

BOOKS IN THE THRIVE PERSONALITY TYPE SERIES

## THRIVE SERIES COLLECTIONS

**The Idealists: Learning To Thrive As, and With, ENFPs, INFPs, ENFJs, and INFJs**

A Collection of Four Books from the Thrive Series.

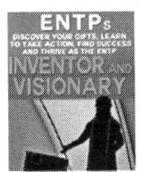

**The Rationals: Learning To Thrive As, and With, The INTJ, ENTJ, INTP, and ENTP Personality Types**

A Collection of Four Books from the Thrive Series.

# ABOUT THE AUTHOR

Dan Johnston is a #1 international best-selling author, speaker, coach, and recognized expert in the fields of confidence, psychology, and personal transformation. As a coach, one of his specialties is helping clients discover their natural talents, apply them to their true purpose, and create a plan of action to live the life of their dreams.

Dan has been a student of psychology, personal change, and social interaction for over a decade. His passion for helping others feel and be their best drives his continuous pursuit to understand exactly how people work.

Dan's educational background includes a degree in Psychology from a world-renowned university, training with Anthony Robbins at his Leadership Academy, and NLP Practitioner Training with Harry Nichols.

In his personal life, Dan has turned his dreams into reality. Between 2012 and 2013 he lived in five new places: Costa Rica, New York, Germany, Italy, and Spain. Today Dan calls Germany his home base but insists that "home" is wherever he hangs his hat for the week. He frequently travels throughout Europe. Dan spends his mornings writing new books and his early evenings on Skype working one-on-one with his coaching clients, supporting them in creating their own dream lives.

**To learn more about Dan Johnston, or inquire about life and business coaching with him, please visit:**

www.DreamsAroundTheWorld.com/coaching

For free articles, interviews, and resources on entrepreneurship, pursuing your passions, travel, and creating the life of your dreams, visit Dreams Around The World and subscribe to the "Business Takeoff Training":

www.DreamsAroundTheWorld.com

**Find more books by Dan Johnston on his Amazon Author Central Pages:**

Amazon.com:

http://www.amazon.com/author/danjohnston

Amazon.co.uk:

http://www.amazon.co.uk/-/e/B00E1DO6OS

# NEVER SETTLE – A SHORT STORY

*This is an article I wrote for revolution. It is on a topic near and dear to my heart. I've included it in this book to let you learn a little bit more about me, and hopefully to inspire you to think big and always go after your dreams. Dan.*

### **Never Settle**

"That is seriously your life? You are literally living the dream. That's insane."

I've grown to expect this every time I tell someone about my fairy-tale of a life. But trust me, it wasn't always this way.

*A lot people put off travel, passions, and happiness until some distant future point; be it the sale of their business, a promotion, or retirement. I used to be one of those procrastinating people.*

I owned my own business and I worked like a dog with the dream of one day "making it." Then I could make happiness a priority. I sacrificed friendships, health, family, and travel opportunities, all because I had to work harder for "just a little while longer." I just needed to "make it" and then things would be different. Then I could I finally start enjoying life.

That was until my business imploded and left me

completely, and I mean completely, broke. To get it started, I needed to co-sign all the business loans and other liabilities, and so when the business failed so did I. Rock bottom occurred. Public failure. Massive financial stress. All that sort of good stuff.

*I can actually remember one night when I was terrified that my date would show up hungry because so much as grabbing a pizza together would mean I couldn't afford pasta and milk the following week. I now refer to this time of my life as my "Pursuit of Happiness" phase.*

But life must go on, right? What was I going to do: marry a government employee, or move to Idaho and get a job as an accountant? Not in this lifetime. And for the record, what the hell does "making it" even mean?!

Fast-forward about 10 months and I'm working as a freelancer and still struggling. It's Saturday evening and the weather is just miserable. Dark clouds, drizzling rain, cold enough to be uncomfortable yet not like a romantic Christmas cold you get bundled up for and almost enjoy. I was at home thinking about my situation and suddenly was overcome with emotions. Where was the light at the end of the tunnel? Something has to change or I'm not going to make it.

I knew I needed to make a serious change in my life

because I couldn't handle the stress much longer. The clear decision was to "Call It Quits" and move back home for a bit. Start applying for jobs, save up a little money, and start rebuilding my life.

*Lucky for me the windows were fogged that night and I wasn't seeing clearly. Fuelled by half a bottle of red wine and a desire to live true to myself and my word, I booked a one-way ticket to Costa Rica.*

Two weeks later, with less than a month's living expenses in the bank and no steady income, I was off to the airport and I had no idea what awaited me on the other side.

It was a huge risk… and it paid off.

The change of scenery reset my emotional clock. The sun beamed energy into my heart and soul. My business grew, like really grew. Four weeks after arriving in Costa Rica, I called my little brother and surprised him with a plane ticket to come visit me the following week. And yes, I could now afford to treat my date to a pepperoni pizza.

This was early 2012. Since then, I've lived in five countries, heading towards my sixth next week (Barcelona, Spain). I've crossed off countless items from my bucket list, including driving a Lamborghini on my birthday, speaking Spanish, playing with a baby monkey, learning to surf, and driving a Hank Moody inspired Porsche up Highway 101.

When things got hard I had plenty of opportunities to raise the white flag. To retreat. To turn my back on the life I really wanted.

*I'm sure you'll have the same opportunities. Ignore them.*

Don't ever, ever think that going for it, going after what you really want, will be easy.

But it will always, always be worth it.

**For More, Visit:**
**www.DreamsAroundTheWorld.com**

Printed in Great Britain
by Amazon.co.uk, Ltd.,
Marston Gate.